EASY GUITAR
WITH NOTES & TAB

Elvis Country Favorites

Cover photo courtesy of Country Music Hall of Fame and Museum

ISBN 978-0-634-01171-9

HAL•LEONARD®
CORPORATION

7777 W. BLUEMOUND RD. P.O. BOX 13819 MILWAUKEE, WI 53213

Visit Hal Leonard Online at
www.halleonard.com
www.elvis-presley.com

STRUM AND PICK PATTERNS

This chart contains the suggested strum and pick patterns that are referred to by number at the beginning of each song in this book. The symbols ⊓ and ∨ in the strum patterns refer to down and up strokes, respectively. The letters in the pick patterns indicate which right-hand fingers plays which strings.

p = thumb
i = index finger
m = middle finger
a = ring finger

For example; Pick Pattern 2
is played: thumb - index - middle - ring

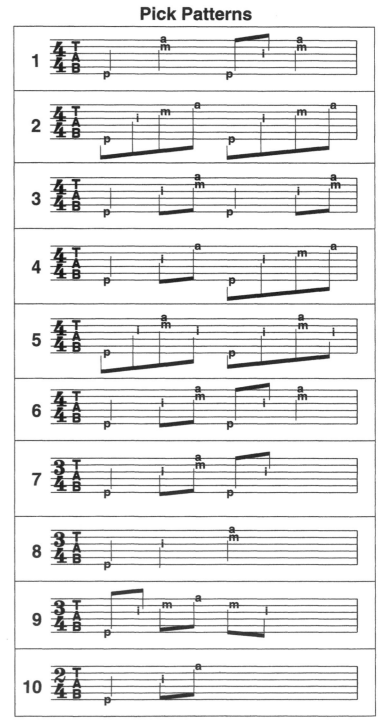

You can use the 3/4 Strum or Pick Patterns in songs written in compound meter (6/8, 9/8, 12/8, etc.).
For example, you can accompany a song in 6/8 by playing the 3/4 pattern twice in each measure.
The 4/4 Strum and Pick Patterns can be used for songs written in cut time (¢) by doubling the note time values in the patterns. Each pattern would therefore last two measures in cut time.

Always on My Mind

Words and Music by Wayne Thompson, Mark James and Johnny Christopher

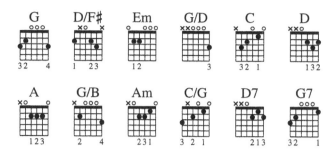

Strum Pattern: 4
Pick Pattern: 3

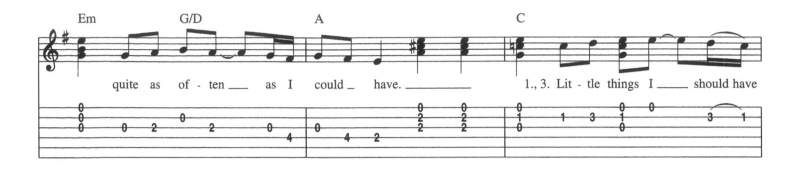

quite as of-ten ___ as I could ___ have. _____ 1., 3. Lit-tle things I ___ should have

said ___ and done, ___ I just ne-ver ___ took the time. _____

Chorus

To Coda ⊕

You were al-ways on my mind; (You were al-ways on my mind.) you were al-ways on my ___

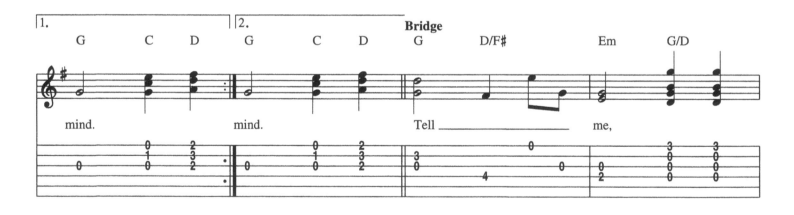

1.   2.   **Bridge**

mind.   mind.   Tell _____ me,

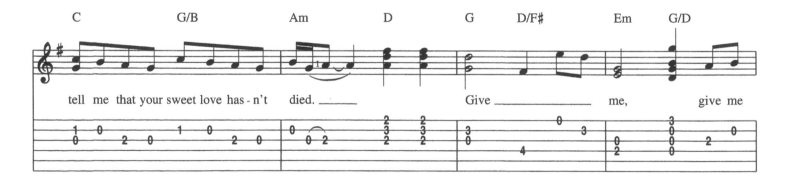

tell me that your sweet love has-n't died. _____ Give _____ me, give me

one more chance to keep you sat - is - fied, _____ sat - is - fied. _____

Coda

mind.) you were al - ways on my mind. _____

Interlude

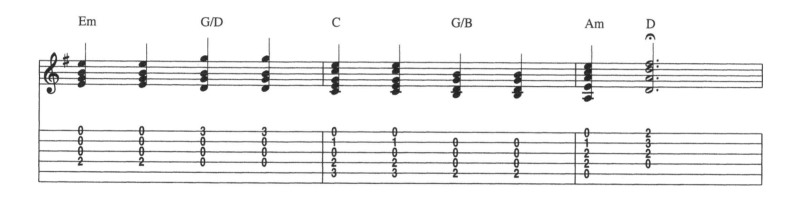

D.S.S. & Fade
(1st Verse)

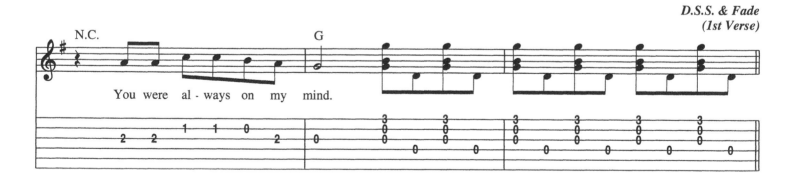

You were al - ways on my mind.

Additional Lyrics

2. Maybe I didn't hold you
   All those lonely, lonely times,
   And I guess I never told you
   I'm so happy that you're mine;
   If I made you feel second best,
   Girl, I'm so sorry I was blind.

Are You Lonesome Tonight?

Words and Music by Roy Turk and Lou Handman

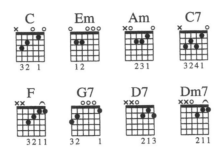

Strum Pattern: 7, 8
Pick Pattern: 8

1. Are you lone - some _ to - night, do you miss me _ to - night, are you sor - ry _ we
2. *Recitation*

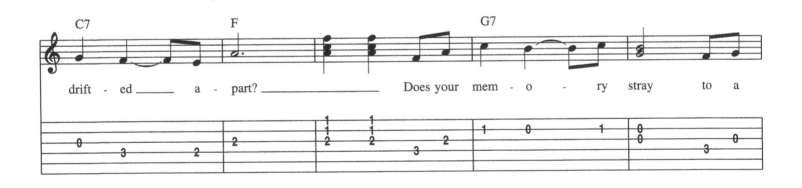

drift - ed _ a - part? _____ Does your mem - o - ry stray to a

bright sum - mer day, when I kissed you and called you _ sweet - heart? _____

Do the chairs in your par - lor ___ seem emp - ty ___ and bare? ___ Do you

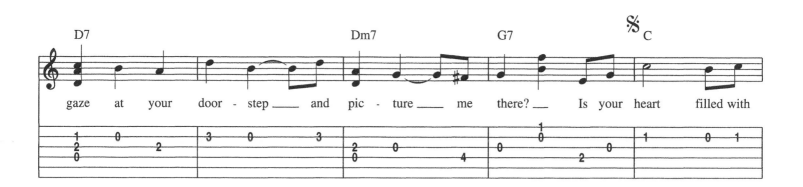

gaze at your door - step ___ and pic - ture ___ me there? ___ Is your heart filled with

To Coda ⊕

pain, shall I come back ___ a - gain? Tell me, dear, are you lone - some ___ to -

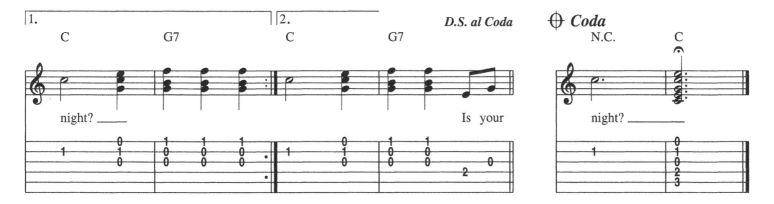

1.
C   G7

2.
C   G7

D.S. al Coda

⊕ **Coda**
N.C.   C

night? ___   Is your   night? ___

Additional Lyrics

Recitation: *I wonder if you're lonesome tonight.*
            You know, someone said that the world's a stage and each must play a part.
            Fate had me playing in love with you as my sweetheart.
            Act one was where we met; I loved you at first glance.
            You read your lines so cleverly and never missed a cue.
            Then came act two, you seemed to change; you acted strange and why I've never known.
            Honey, you lied when you said you loved me,
            And I had no cause to doubt you.
            But I'd rather go on hearing your lies,
            Than to go on living without you.
            Now the stage is bare and I'm standing there with emptiness all around.
            And if you won't come back to me, then they can bring the curtain down.

Blue Eyes Crying in the Rain

Words and Music by Fred Rose

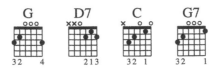

Strum Pattern: 4
Pick Pattern: 3

Verse
Moderately Slow

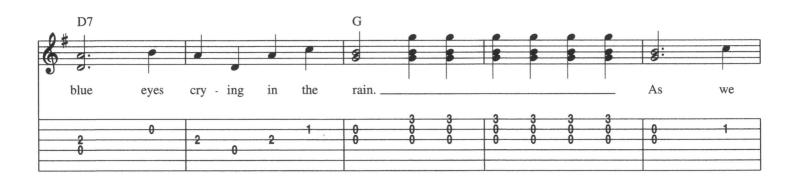

1. In the twi - light glow I see her, ___ blue eyes cry - ing in the rain. ___ As we
2. *See Additional Lyrics*

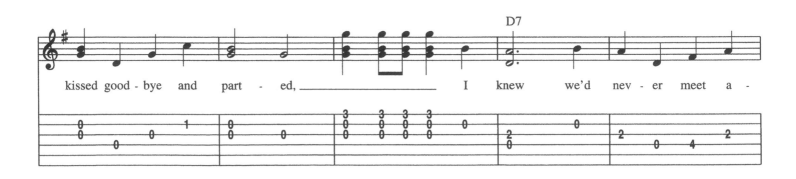

kissed good - bye and part - ed, ___ I knew we'd nev - er meet a -

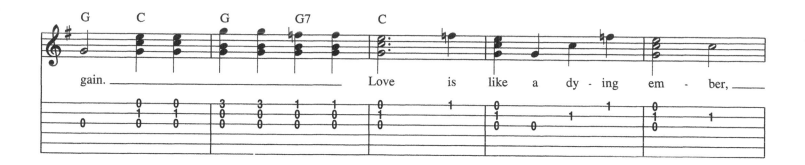

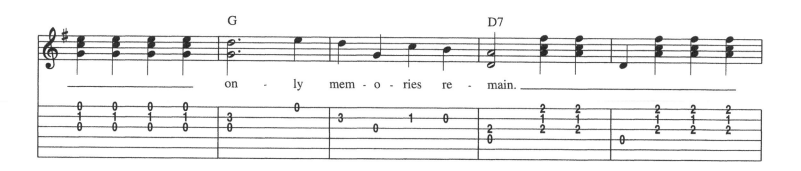

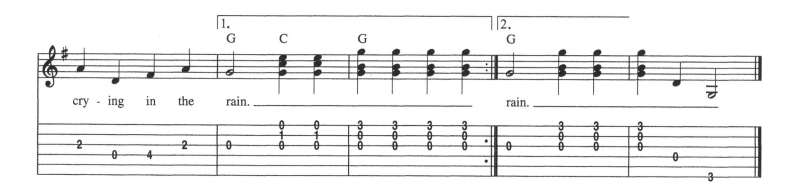

Additional Lyrics

2. Now my hair has turned to silver,
All my life I've loved in vain.
I can see her star in heaven,
Blue eyes crying in the rain.
Someday when we meet up yonder,
We'll stroll hand in hand again.
In a land that knows no parting,
Blue eyes crying in the rain.

Blue Moon of Kentucky

Words and Music by Bill Monroe

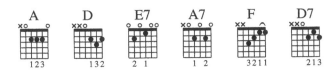

Strum Pattern: 6
Pick Pattern: 4

Intro
Moderately Fast

Blue moon.   Blue moon.   Blue moon

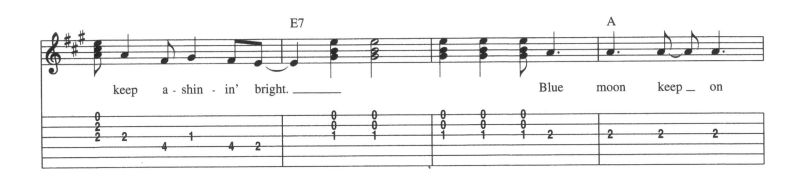

keep a - shin - in' bright. _____   Blue moon keep __ on

shin - in' bright, __ you're gon - na bring me back __ a - my ba - by to - night. __ Blue

moon keep a-shin-in' bright. __ 1. I said blue

%% **Chorus**

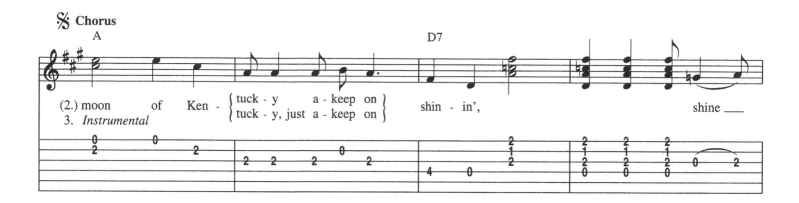

(2.) moon of Ken- { tuck-y a-keep on } shin-in', shine __
3. *Instrumental* { tuck-y, just a-keep on }

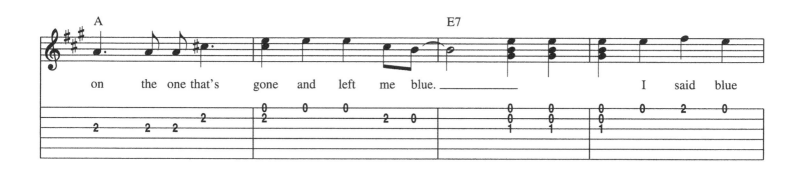

on the one that's gone and left me blue. _____ I said blue

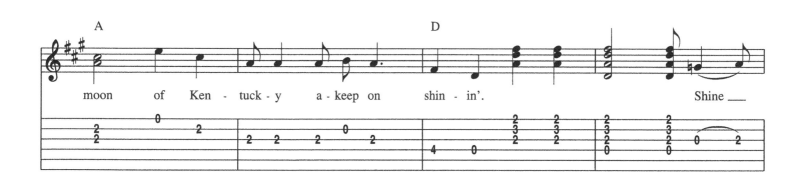

moon of Ken-tuck-y a-keep on shin-in'. Shine __

To Coda 1 ⊕

on the one that's gone __ and left me blue. _____ Well-a it was

Bridge

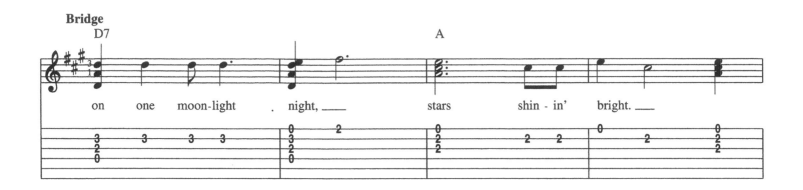

on one moon-light night, ____ stars shin-in' bright. ____

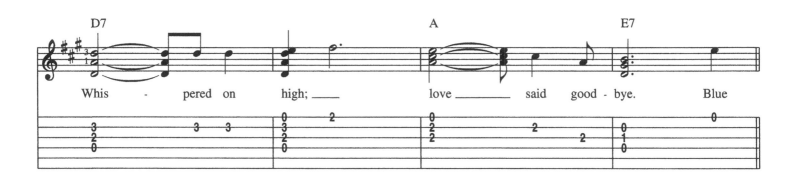

Whis - pered on high; ____ love ____ said good - bye. Blue

Outro-Chorus

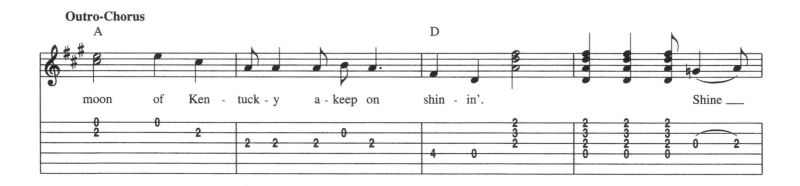

moon of Ken - tuck - y a - keep on shin - in'. Shine ____

To Coda 2 ⊕   *D.S. al Coda 1*

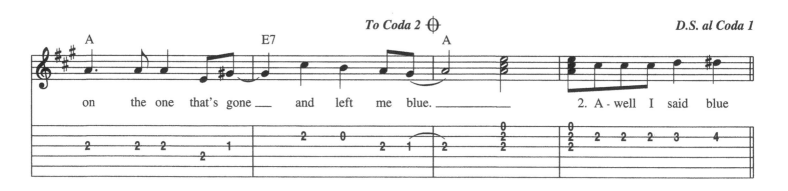

on the one that's gone ____ and left me blue. ____ 2. A - well I said blue

⊕ *Coda 1*   *D.S. al Coda 2*   ⊕ *Coda 2*

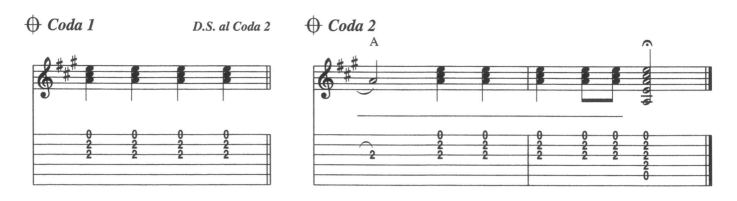

Don't Cry Daddy

Words and Music by Mac Davis

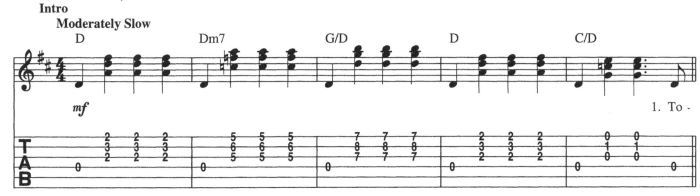

Strum Pattern: 1, 2
Pick Pattern: 2, 4

Intro
Moderately Slow

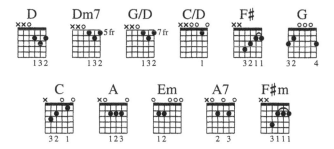

day I stum-bled from _ my bed, with thun-der crash-ing in ___ my head, my
2. See Additional Lyrics

pil-low still wet from last night's tears. _____ And

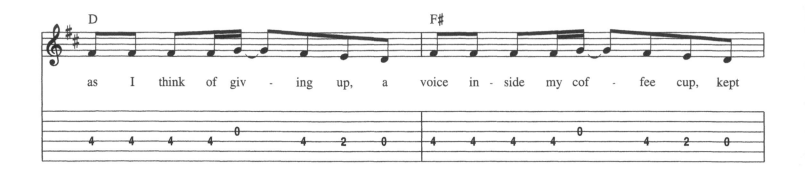

as I think of giv - ing up, a voice in - side my cof - fee cup, kept

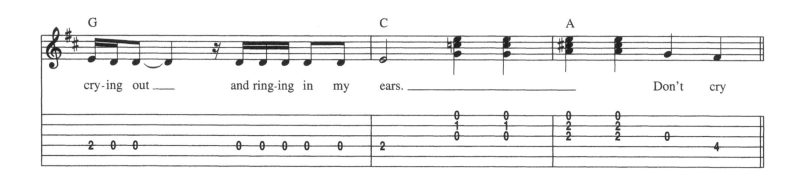

cry-ing out ____ and ring-ing in my ears. _____ Don't cry

Chorus

Dad - dy, _____ Dad-dy, please don't cry. _____ Dad-dy,

you've still got me and lit - tle Tom - my, to - geth - er we'll find a brand ____ new mom - my.

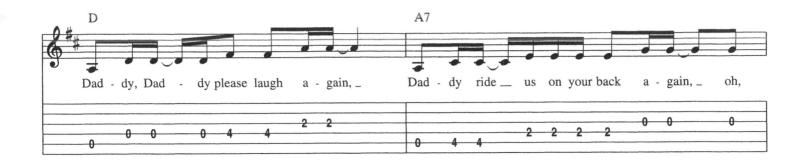

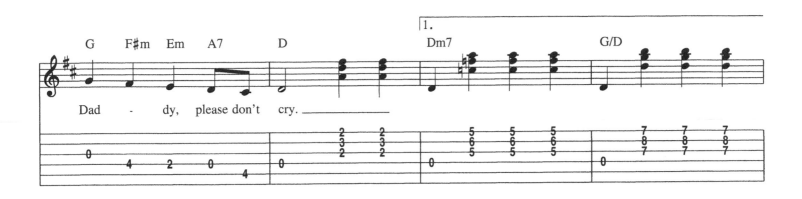

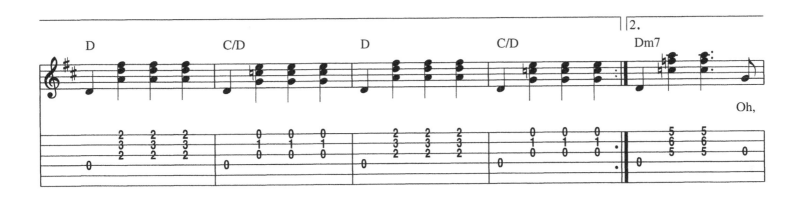

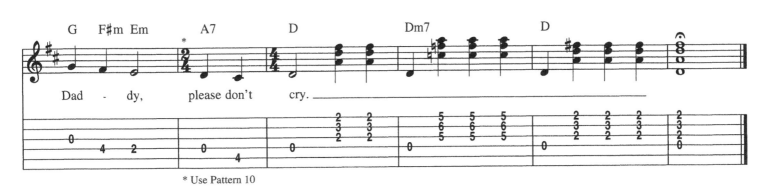

* Use Pattern 10

Additional Lyrics

2. Why are children always first
   To feel the pain and hurt the worst,
   It's true, but somehow it just don't seem right.
   'Cause ev'rytime I cry I know it hurts my little children so,
   I wonder will it be the same tonight.

For the Good Times

Words and Music by Kris Kristofferson

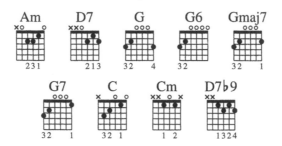

Strum Pattern: 3
Pick Pattern: 3

1. Don't look so sad; I know it's o-ver. But life goes

2. *See Additional Lyrics*

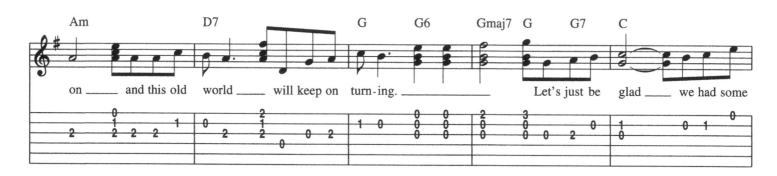

on and this old world will keep on turn-ing. Let's just be glad we had some

time to spend to-geth-er. There's no need to watch the bridg-es that we're

burn-ing. Lay your head up-on my pil-low, hold your

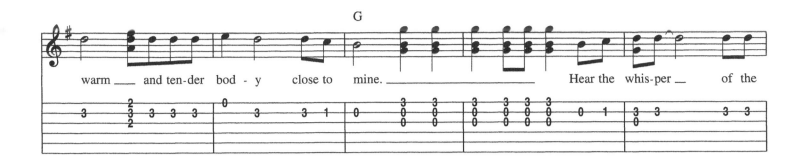

warm ___ and ten-der bod-y   close to   mine. _____   Hear the   whis-per ___   of the

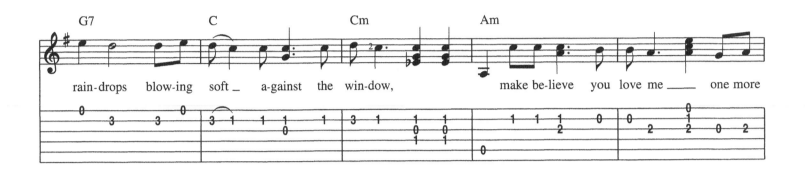

rain-drops   blow-ing   soft ___   a-gainst   the   win-dow,   make be-lieve   you   love me ___   one more

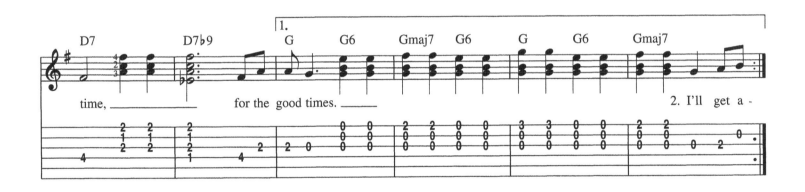

time, _____   for the   good times. _____   2. I'll   get a -

good times, _____   for the   good times. _____   *rit.*

Additional Lyrics

2. I'll get along; you'll find another;
And I'll be here if you should find you ever need me.
Don't say a word about tomorrow or forever.
There'll be time enough for sadness when you leave me.

From a Jack to a

Words and Music by Ned Miller

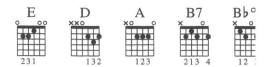

Strum Pattern: 4
Pick Pattern: 3

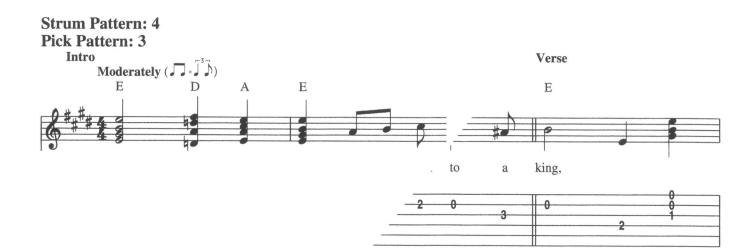

*wedding ring

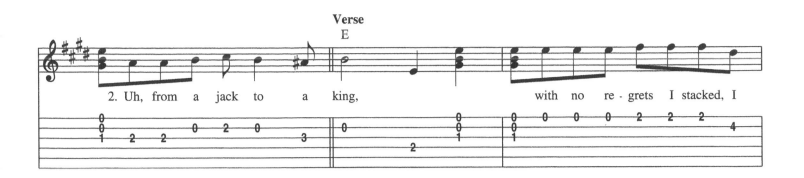

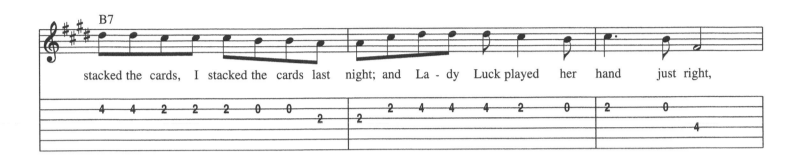

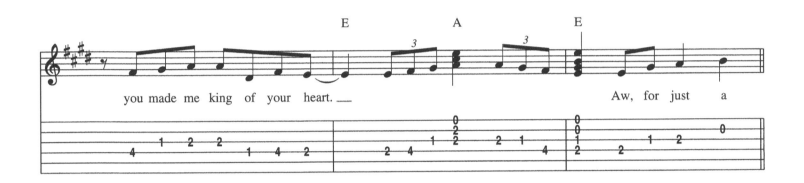

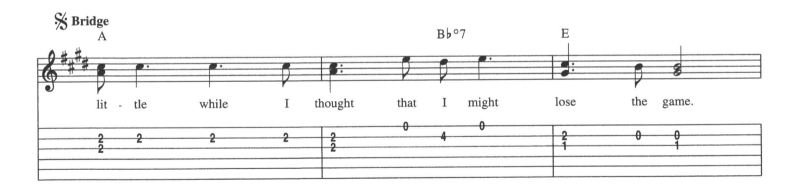

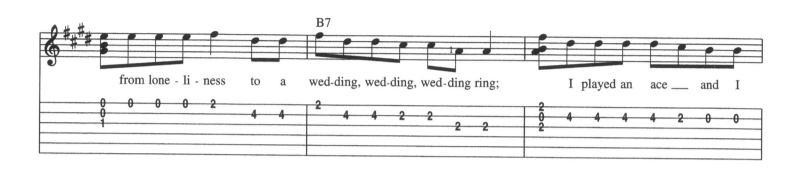

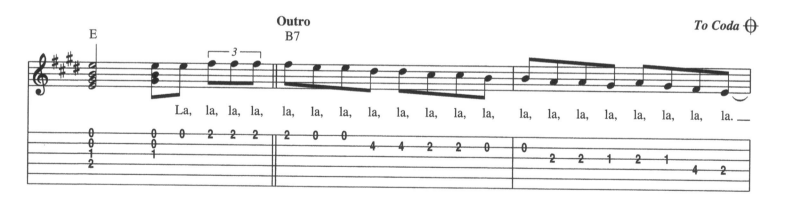

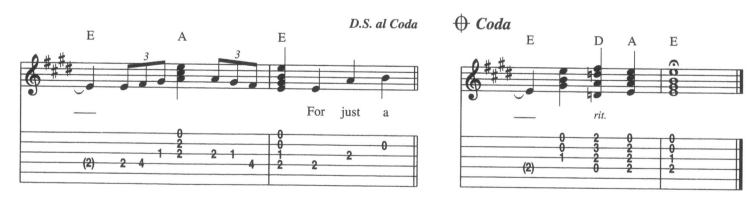

I'm So Lonesome I Could Cry

Words and Music by Hank Williams

Strum Pattern: 4
Pick Pattern: 3

1. Hear ___ that lone - some whip - poor - will, ___ he sounds ___ too blue ___ to fly. ___
2., 3. *See Additional Lyrics*

___ The mid - night train ___ is whin - ing low. ___ I'm so lone - some I ___ could ___

cry. ___ 2. Did you cry. ___ I'm so lone - some I ___ could ___ cry. ___

Additional Lyrics

2. Did you ever see a robin weep
   When leaves began to die?
   That means he's lost the will to live.
   I'm so lonesome I could cry.

3. The silence of a falling star
   Lights up a purple sky.
   And as I wonder where you are
   I'm so lonesome I could cry.
   I'm so lonesome I could cry.

Funny How Time Slips Away

Words and Music by Willie Nelson

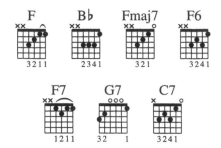

Strum Pattern: 2, 3
Pick Pattern: 4

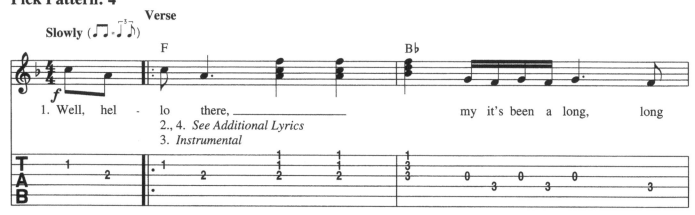

1. Well, hel - lo there, _____ my it's been a long, long

2., 4. See Additional Lyrics
3. Instrumental

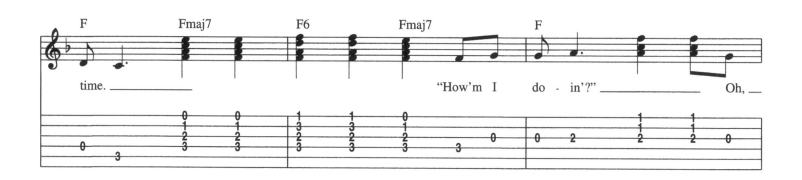

time. _____ "How'm I do - in'?" _____ Oh, ___

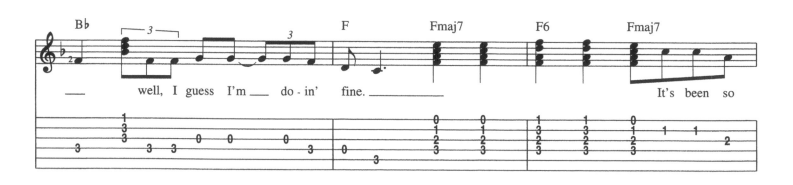

___ well, I guess I'm ___ do - in' fine. _____ It's been so

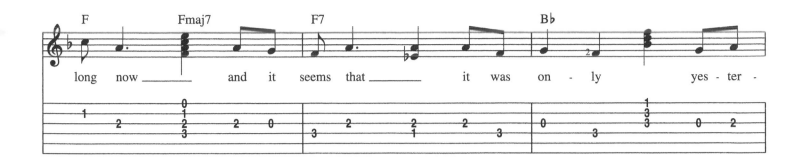

long now _____ and it seems that _____ it was on - ly yes - ter -

day. _____ Mm, _____ ain't it fun - ny _____ how time slips a -

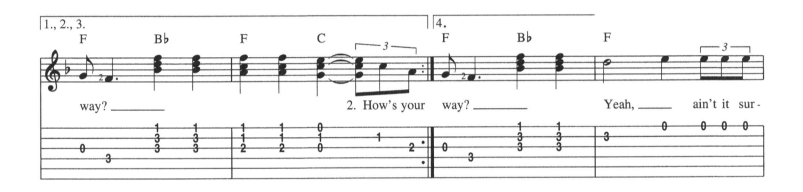

way? _____ 2. How's your way? _____ Yeah, _____ ain't it sur -

pris - in' how time slips _ a - way? _____

Additional Lyrics

2. How's your new love,
   I hope that he's doin' fine.
   Heard you told him, yes baby,
   That you'd love him till the end of time.
   Well, you know that's the same thing that you told me,
   Well, it seems like just the other day.
   Mm, ain't it funny how time slips away?

4. Gotta go now,
   Guess I'll see you hangin' 'round.
   Don't know when though, oh no,
   Never know when I'll be back in town.
   But I remember what I told you,
   That in time you gonna pay.
   Ain't it surprisin' how time slips away?
   Yeah, ain't it surprisin' how time slips away?

Green Green Grass of Home

Words and Music by Curly Putman

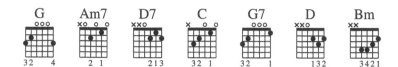

Strum Pattern: 4
Pick Pattern: 3

Intro
Moderately Slow

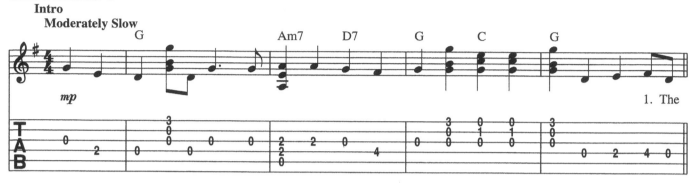

mp

1. The

Verse

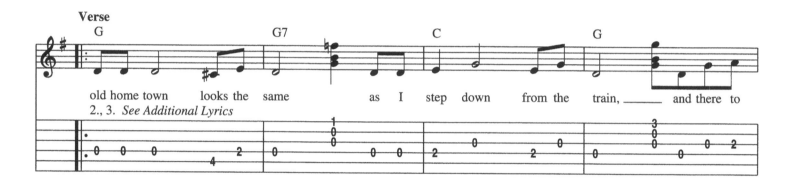

old home town looks the same as I step down from the train, _____ and there to
2., 3. *See Additional Lyrics*

meet me is my ma-ma and my pa-pa.

Down the

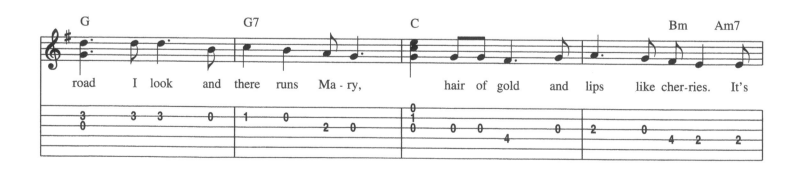

road I look and there runs Ma-ry, hair of gold and lips like cher-ries. It's

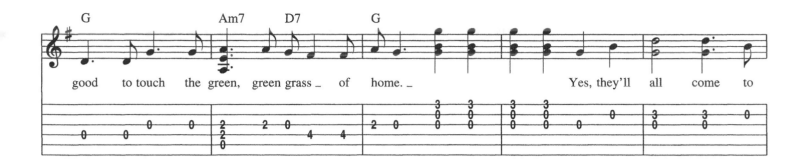

good to touch the green, green grass _ of home. _ Yes, they'll all come to

1., 2. meet me, ____ arms _ reach-ing, ____ smil-ing sweet-ly; oh, it's good to touch the
3. see me ____ in the

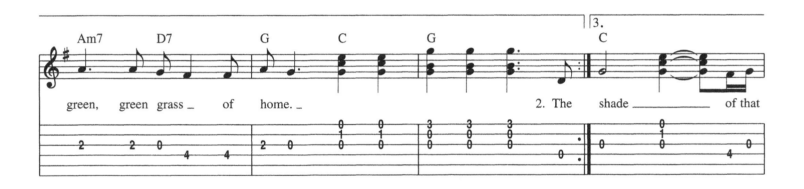

green, green grass _ of home. _ 2. The shade _____ of that

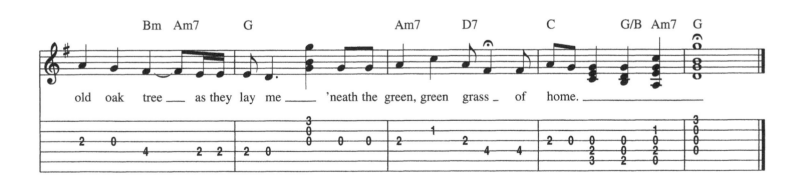

old oak tree ____ as they lay me ____ 'neath the green, green grass _ of home. ____

Additional Lyrics

2. The old house is still standing
   Tho' the paint is cracked and dry,
   And there's that old oak tree
   That I used to play on.
   Down the lane I walk with my sweet Mary,
   Hair of gold and lips like cherries.
   It's good to touch the green, green grass of home.

3. *Spoken:* *Then I awake and look around me*
   At four gray walls that surround me
   Sung: And I realize that I was only dreaming.
   For there's a guard and there's a sad old padre,
   Arm in arm we'll walk at daybreak.
   Again I'll touch the green, green grass of home.

Help Me Make It Through the Night

Words and Music by Kris Kristofferson

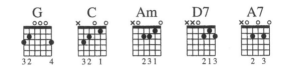

Strum Pattern: 4
Pick Pattern: 3, 4

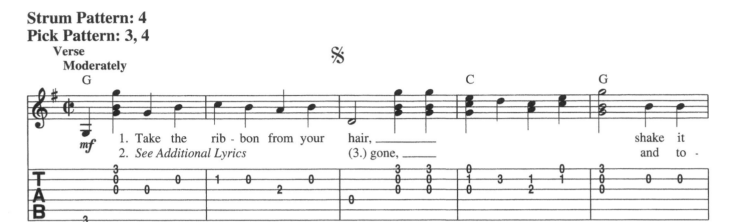

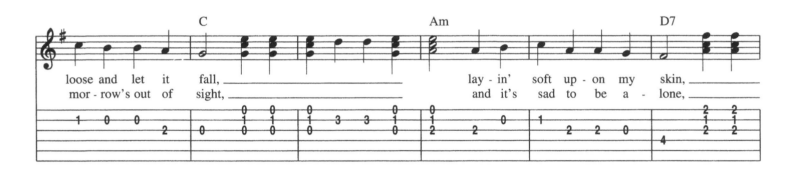

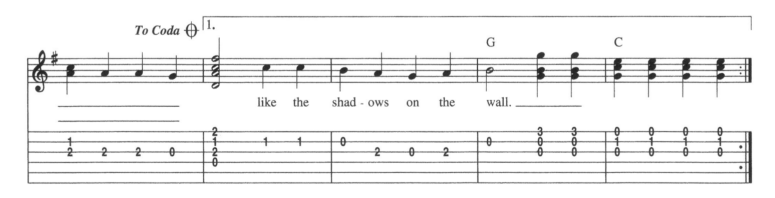

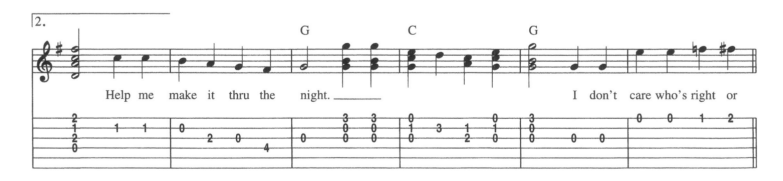

Bridge

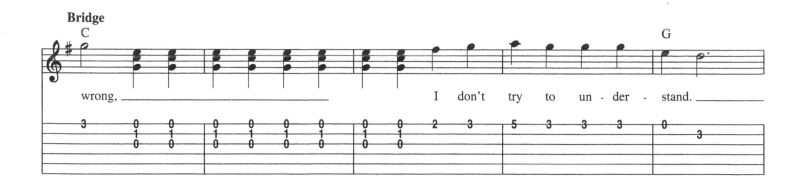

wrong, _____ I don't try to un - der - stand. _____

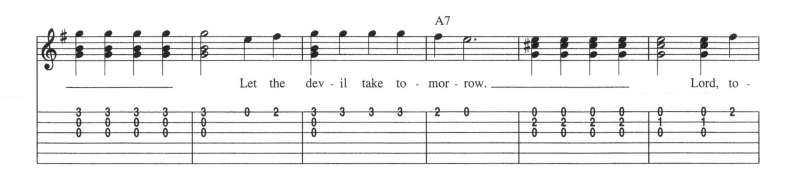

_____ Let the dev - il take to - mor - row. _____ Lord, to -

D.S. al Coda

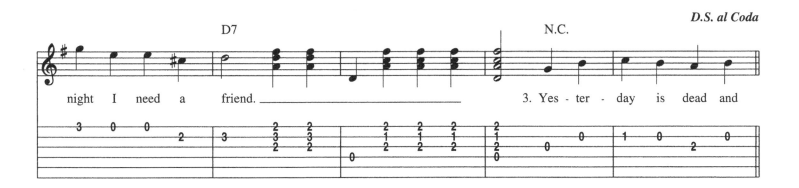

night I need a friend. _____ 3. Yes - ter - day is dead and

⊕ *Coda*

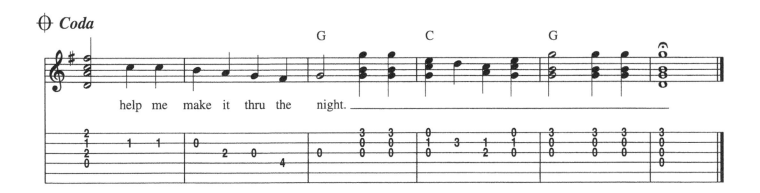

help me make it thru the night. _____

Additional Lyrics

2. Come and lay down by my side
   Till the early mornin' light.
   All I'm takin' is your time.
   Help me make it thru the night.

I Can't Stop Loving You

Words and Music by Don Gibson

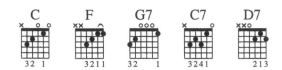

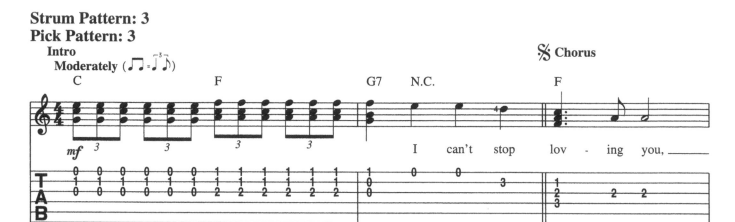

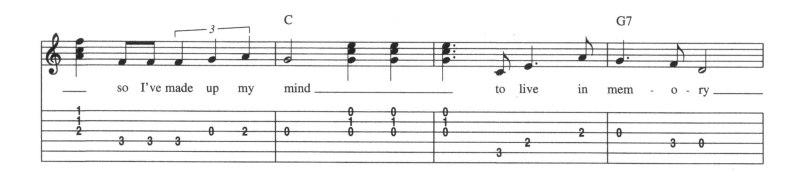

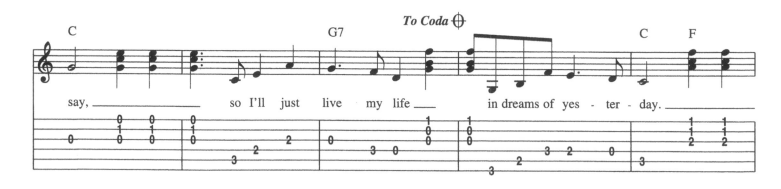

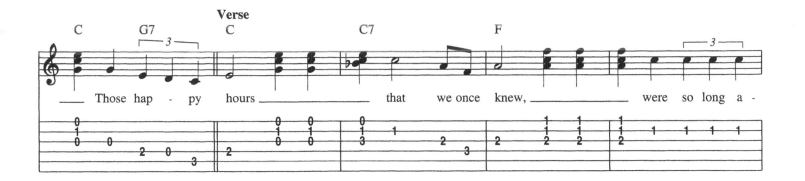

Those hap - py hours _____ that we once knew, _____ were so long a -

go, _____ but they still make, _ make me blue. _____ They say _ that

time _____ heals a bro - ken heart, _____ but time has stood

D.S. al Coda

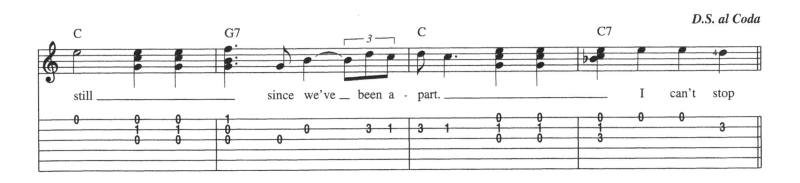

still _____ since we've _ been a - part. _____ I can't stop

⊕ *Coda*

in dreams of yes - ter - day, _ yes - ter - day, _ yes - ter - day. _

I Forgot to Remember to Forget

Words and Music by Stanley A. Kesler and Charlie Feathers

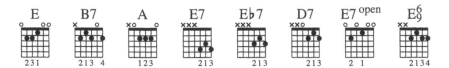

Strum Pattern: 4
Pick Pattern: 2

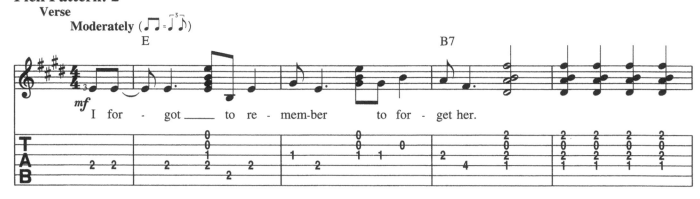

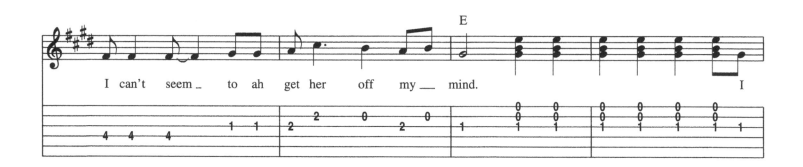

I for - got ___ to re - mem - ber to for - get her.

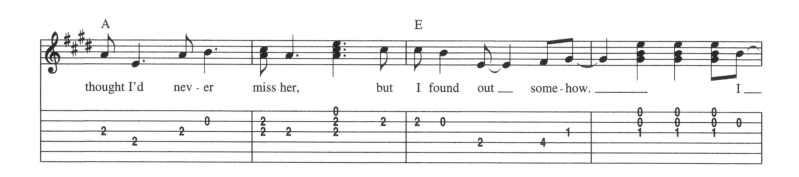

I can't seem ___ to ah get her off my ___ mind.

thought I'd nev - er miss her, but I found out ___ some - how. ___ I ___

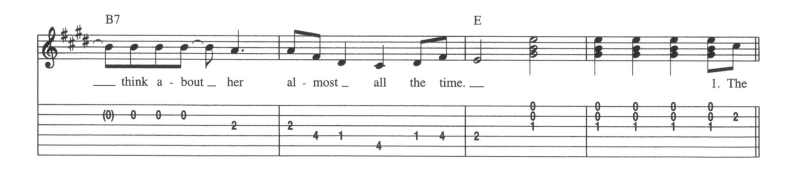

___ think a - bout ___ her al - most ___ all the time. ___ 1. The

Chorus

(3.) day she went a - way, ___ I made my - self a prom - ise _____
2. *Instrumental*

that I'd soon ___ for - get we ev - er met. _____ { But / Well, but }

some - thing sure is wrong _ 'cause I'm so blue _ and lone - ly I ___ for -

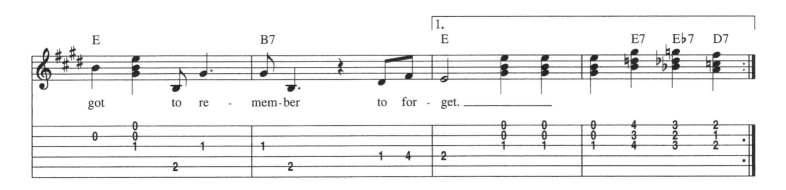

got to re - mem - ber to for - get. _____

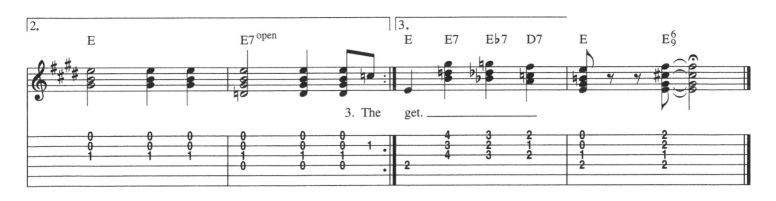

3. The get. _____

It's a Matter of Time

Words and Music by Clive Westlake

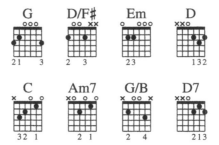

Strum Pattern: 2
Pick Pattern: 4

Intro
Moderately

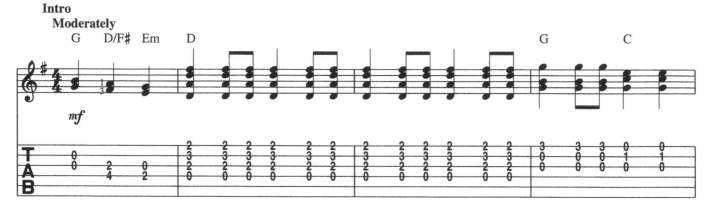

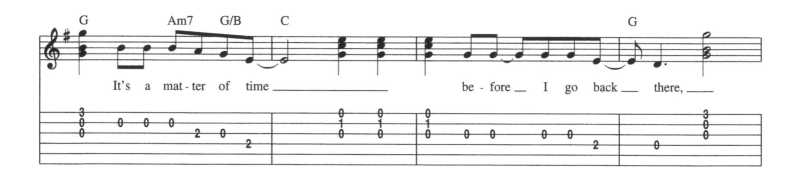

It's a mat-ter of time _____ be-fore __ I go back __ there, _____

a mat-ter of time _____ be-fore I go home. ____ 1. I have

been ____ 'way from her ___ now ___ for a long ___ time ____ an' I've lived __

2. See Additional Lyrics

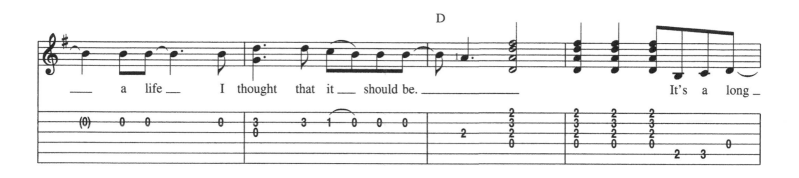

__ a life __ I thought that it ___ should be. _____ It's a long __

__ long way from now to ___ may-be some - time _____ and the wait -

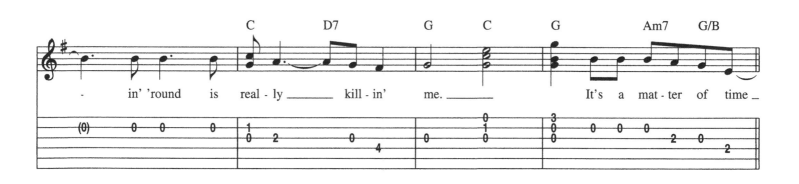

- in' 'round is real-ly _____ kill-in' me. _____ It's a mat-ter of time __

Chorus

_____ be - fore __ I go back __ there, ____ a mat-ter of time, __

oh Lord, be-fore I go home. It's a long way, I

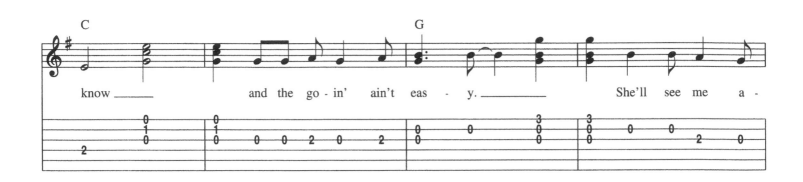

know and the go-in' ain't eas-y. She'll see me a-

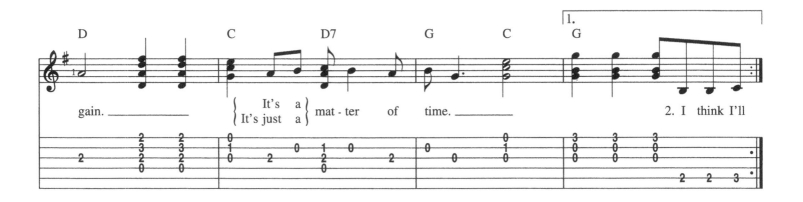

gain. It's a / It's just a mat-ter of time. 2. I think I'll

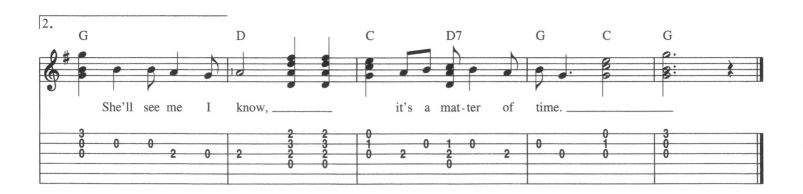

She'll see me I know, it's a mat-ter of time.

Additional Lyrics

2. I think I'll take a train right early in the morning
   Just to see how far I'll get along the way.
   But the trains don't run too often, only sometime;
   So I guess I'd better wait another day.

Kentucky Rain

Words and Music by Eddie Rabbitt and Dick Heard

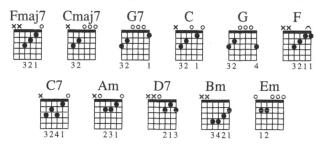

Strum Pattern: 3, 4
Pick Pattern: 3

Intro
Slowly

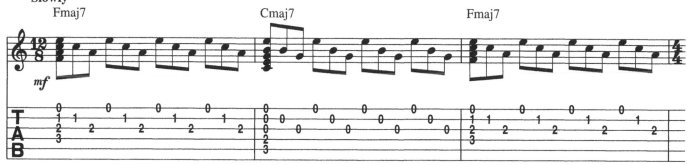

Verse

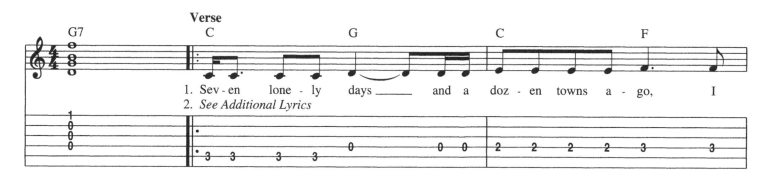

1. Sev-en lone-ly days _____ and a doz-en towns a-go, I
2. *See Additional Lyrics*

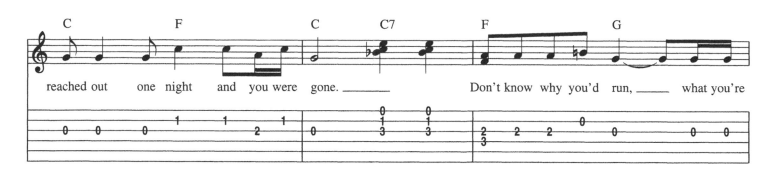

reached out one night and you were gone. _____ Don't know why you'd run, _____ what you're

run-nin' to or from, _____ all I know _____ is I want to bring you

home. _____ So I'm walk - ing _____ in the rain _____

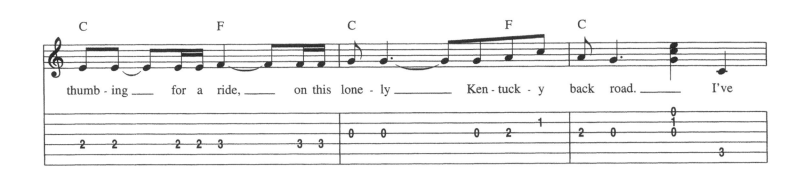

thumb - ing _____ for a ride, _____ on this lone - ly _____ Ken - tuck - y back road. _____ I've

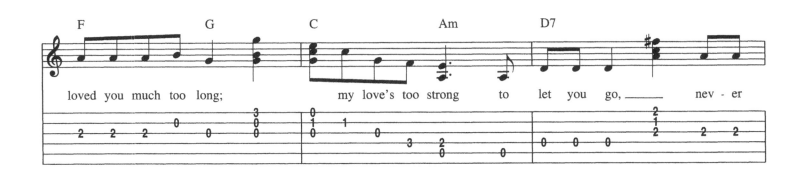

loved you much too long; my love's too strong to let you go, _____ nev - er

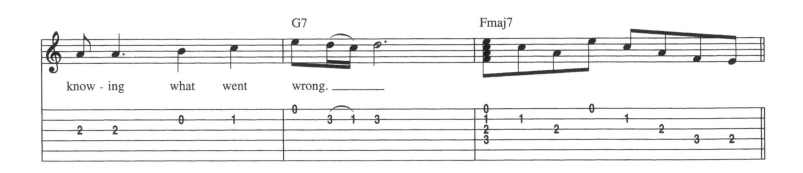

know - ing what went wrong. _____

Chorus

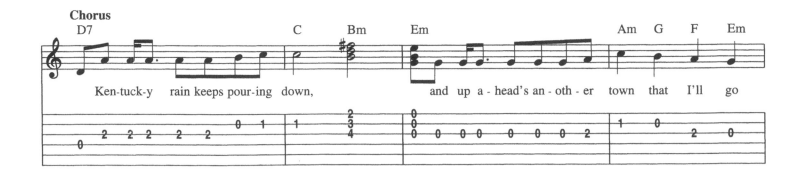

Ken-tuck-y rain keeps pour-ing down, and up a - head's an - oth - er town that I'll go

walk-ing through, ___ with the rain in my shoes, ___ (Rain in my shoes.)

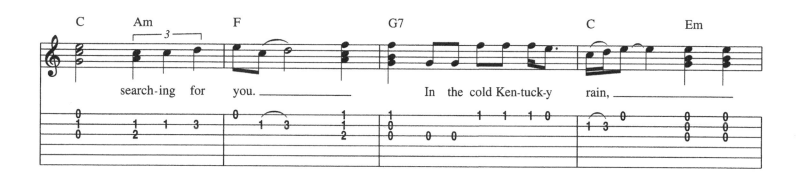

search-ing for you. ___ In the cold Ken-tuck-y rain, ___

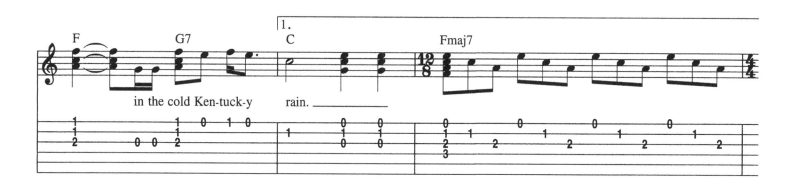

1.

in the cold Ken-tuck-y rain. ___

2.

Repeat & Fade

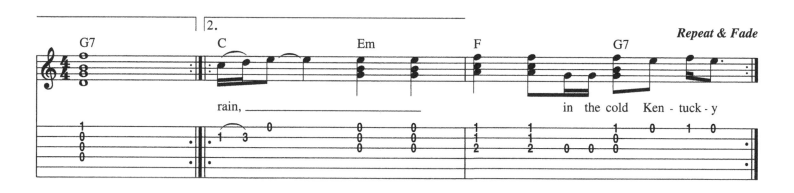

rain, ___ in the cold Ken - tuck - y

Additional Lyrics

2. Showed your photograph to some old gray-bearded men
   Sitting on a bench outside a gen'ral store;
   They said, "Yes, she's been here," but their mem'ry wasn't clear,
   Was it yesterday, no wait, the day before.
   Fin'ly got a ride with a preacher man who asked,
   "Where you bound on such a cold dark afternoon?"
   As we drove on through the rain, as he listened, I explained,
   And he left me with a prayer that I'd find you.

Just for Old Time's Sake

Words and Music by Sid Tepper and Roy C. Bennett

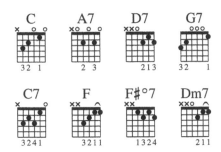

Strum Pattern: 7, 8
Pick Pattern: 7, 8

Verse
Slowly

Just for old time's sake, won't you give my heart a break?

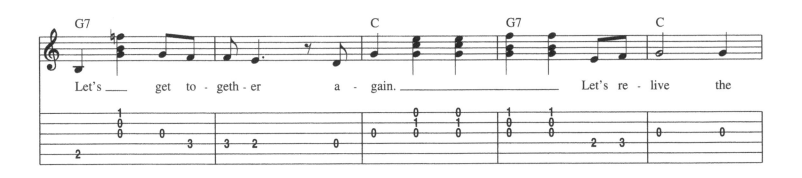

Let's ___ get to-geth-er a - gain. _____ Let's re-live the

time I was yours and you were mine. _____ Life ___ was so won-der-ful ___

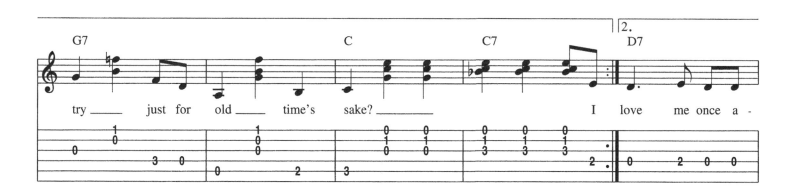

Little Sister

Words and Music by Doc Pomus and Mort Shuman

Strum Pattern: 2, 3
Pick Pattern: 3, 4

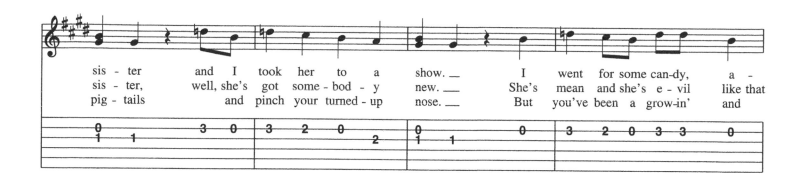

sis - ter　　and I took her to a　show. ___　　I went for some can-dy,　a -
sis - ter,　well, she's got some - bod - y　new. ___　　She's mean and she's e - vil　like that
pig - tails　and pinch your turned - up　nose. ___　　But you've been a grow-in'　and

1., 2., 3.
3rd time, D.S. al Coda

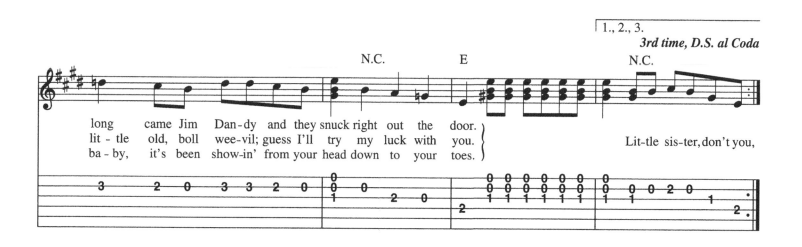

N.C.　　　　　E　　　　　N.C.

long　came Jim Dan-dy and they snuck right out the door.
lit - tle old, boll wee-vil; guess I'll try my luck with you.
ba - by,　it's been show-in' from your head down to your toes.

Lit-tle sis-ter, don't you,

Coda

E　　　　　B7　　　C7　　B7

done.　　　　　Lit-tle sis-ter, don't you　do what your big　sis-ter

1.　E　　　　　　　　　2.　E

done.　　　　　done.

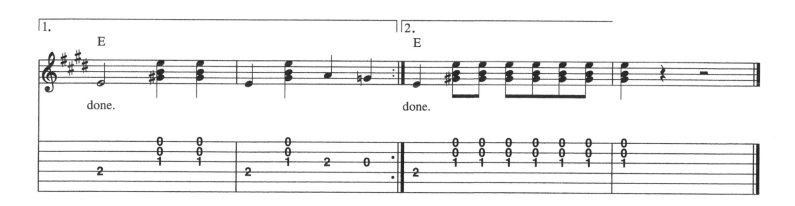

Make the World Go Away

Words and Music by Hank Cochran

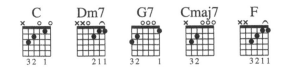

Strum Pattern: 3, 4
Pick Pattern: 3

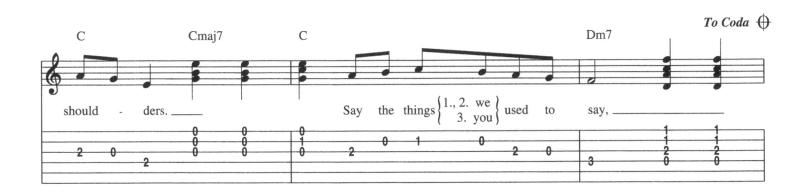

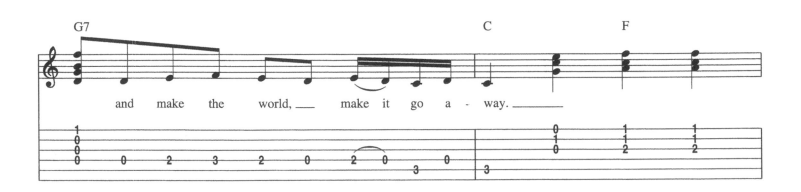

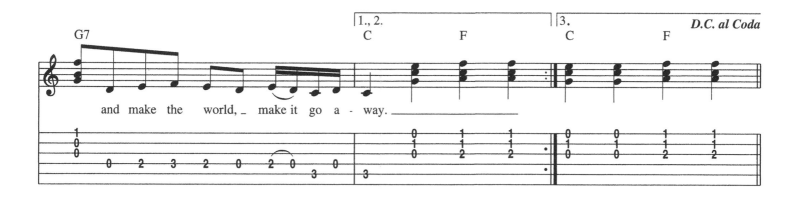

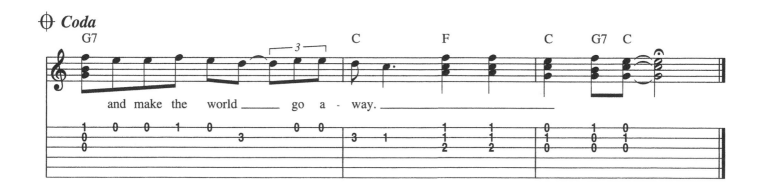

Additional Lyrics

2. Now I'm sorry if I hurt you,
   Let me make it up to you day by day.
   And if you will, please forgive me,
   And make the world, make it go away.

Mystery Train

Words and Music by Sam C. Phillips and Herman Parker Jr.

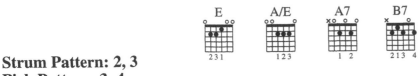

Strum Pattern: 2, 3
Pick Pattern: 3, 4

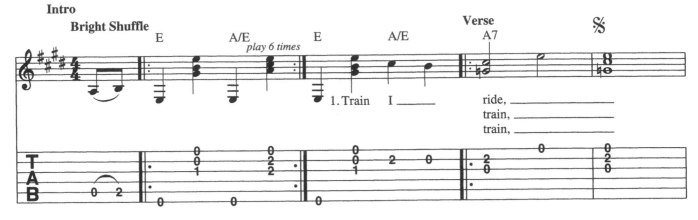

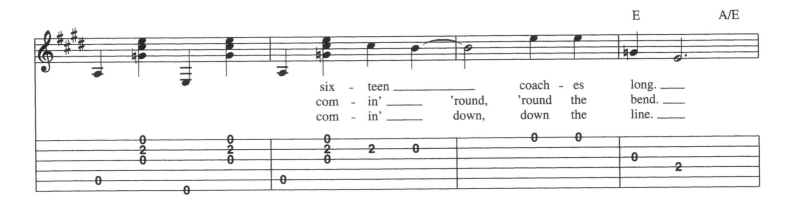

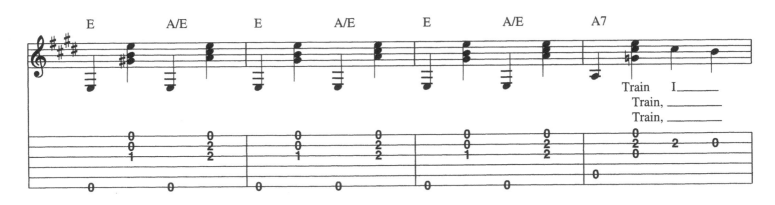

Release Me

Words and Music by Robert Yount, Eddie Miller and Dub Williams

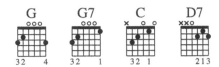

Strum Pattern: 3, 4
Pick Pattern: 3

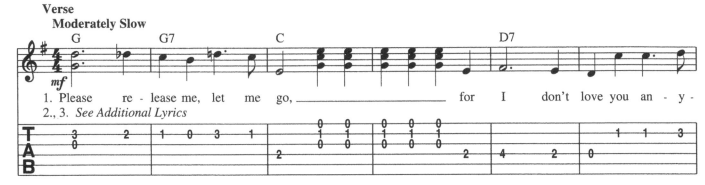

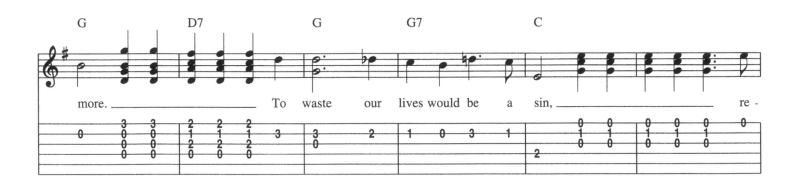

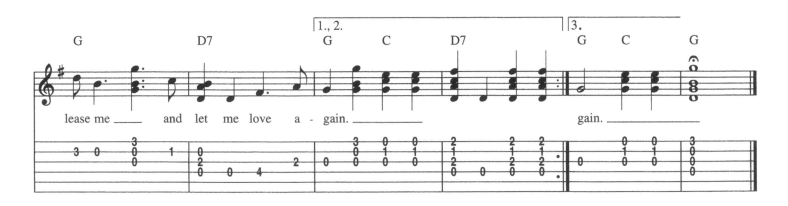

Additional Lyrics

2. I have found a new love, dear,
   And I will always want her near.
   Her lips are warm while yours are cold.
   Release me, my darling, let me go.

3. Please release me, can't you see,
   You'd be a fool to cling to me.
   To live a lie would bring us pain,
   So release me and let me love again.

You Gave Me a Mountain

Words and Music by Marty Robbins

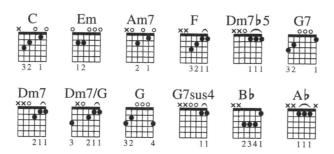

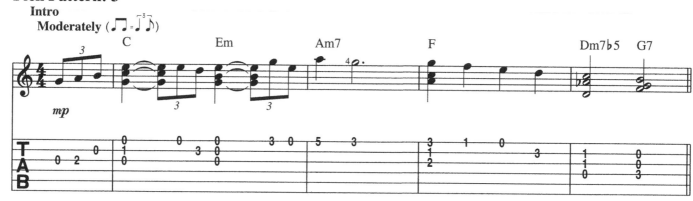

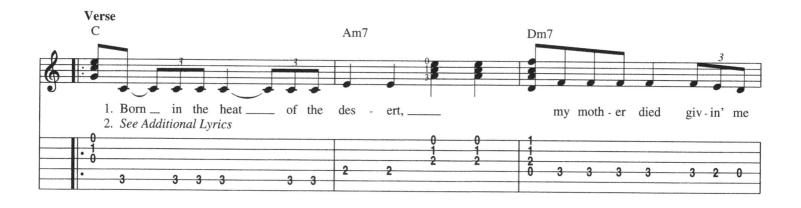

47

blamed _ for the loss _____ of his wife. You know, Lord, I've been _____ in a

pris - on, _____ for some - thing that I've _____ nev - er done. _____

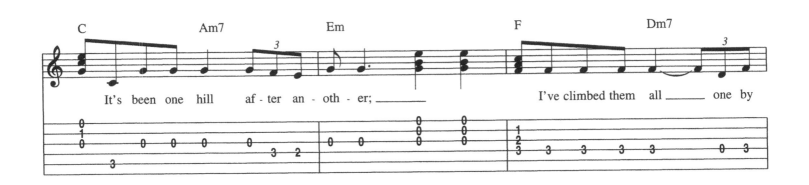

It's been one hill af - ter an - oth - er; _____ I've climbed them all _____ one by

Chorus

one. _____ Oh, but this time, _ Lord, you gave me _____ a moun - tain, _____ a

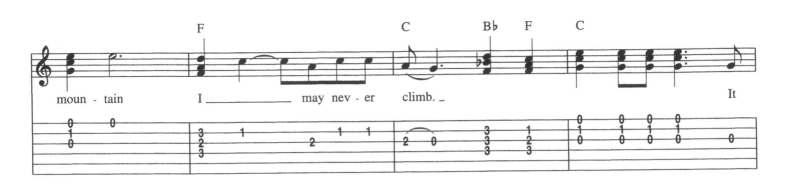

moun - tain I _____ may nev - er climb. _ It

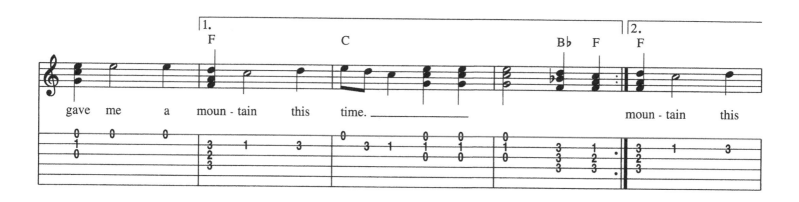

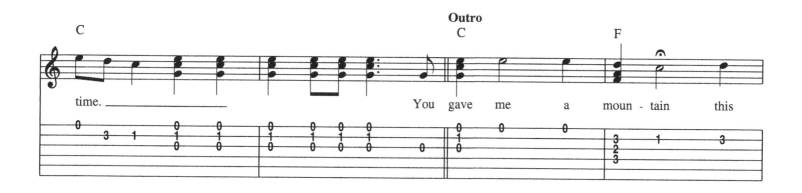

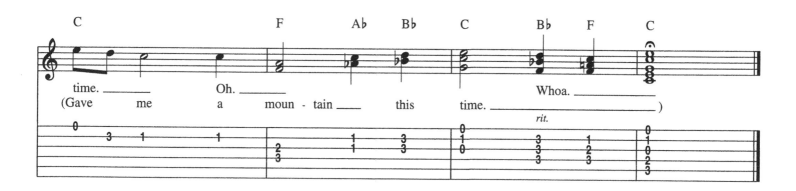

Additional Lyrics

2. My woman got tired of the heartaches,
   Tired of the grief and the strife.
   So tired of workin' for nothin',
   Just tired of being my wife.
   She took my one ray of sunshine,
   She took my pride and my joy.
   She took my reason for living,
   She took my small baby boy.

She's Not You

Words and Music by Doc Pomus, Jerry Leiber and Mike Stoller

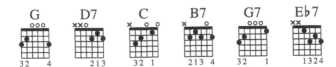

G   D7   C   B7   G7   Eb7

Strum Pattern: 3
Pick Pattern: 3

Verse
Moderately

Her hair is soft and her eyes are, oh, so blue. ___ She's all the

things a girl should be, but she's not you. ___ She knows just how to make me

laugh when I feel blue. ___ She's ev-'ry-thing a man could want, but she's not

you. ___ And when we're danc - ing, it al-most

feels the same. ___ I've got to stop my-self from whis-p'ring your name. She e - ven

To Coda ⊕

Outro

kiss - es me like you used to do. _____ And it's just break - ing my heart 'cause she's not

Interlude

you. _____

D.S. al Coda

And it's just break - ing my heart 'cause she's not you. _____

⊕ **Coda**

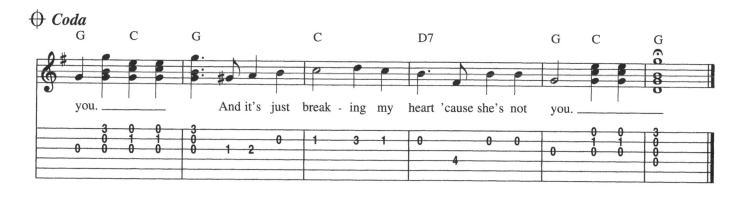

you. _____ And it's just break - ing my heart 'cause she's not you. _____

Snowbird

Words and Music by Gene MacLellan

Strum Pattern: 4, 5
Pick Pattern: 3

%. **Verse**

Brightly

1. Be - neath this snow-y man-tle cold and clean, _____ the un-born grass lies wait-ing for its
2., 3. *See Additional Lyrics*

coat to turn to green. _____ The snow-bird sings the song he al - ways sings, _____ and

speaks to me _ of flow - ers that will bloom a - gain _ in spring. _____ 2. When _____

Chorus

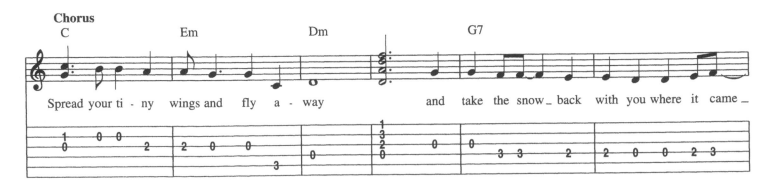

Spread your ti - ny wings and fly a - way and take the snow _ back with you where it came _

from on that day. The one I love for-ev-er is un-true, _____

_and if I could, you know that I ___ would fly a-way with you. _____ 3. The_

To Coda ⊕   *D.S. al Coda*
(take 2nd ending)

⊕ **Coda**

_Yeah, ___ if I could _ you know _ that I would fly _____

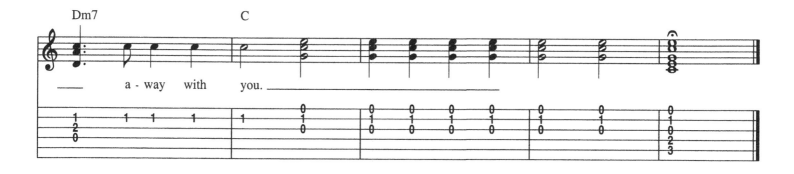

_a-way with you. _____

Additional Lyrics

2. When I was young my heart was young then too,
   Anything that it would tell me
   That's the thing that I would do.
   But now I feel such emptiness within
   For the thing I want the most in life
   Is the thing that I can't win.

3. The breeze along the river seems to say,
   That she'll only break my heart again
   Should I decide to stay.
   So little snowbird take me with you when you go
   To that land of gentle breezes
   Where the peaceful waters flow.

That's All Right

Words and Music by Arthur Crudup

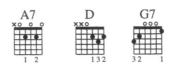

Strum Pattern: 3, 4
Pick Pattern: 3, 5

Moderately Bright

1. Well,

Verse

that's	all	right, _____	ma - ma,	that's	all	right	for
2. ma - ma	she	done	told me,	pa - pa	done	told	me

3., 4. *See Additional Lyrics*

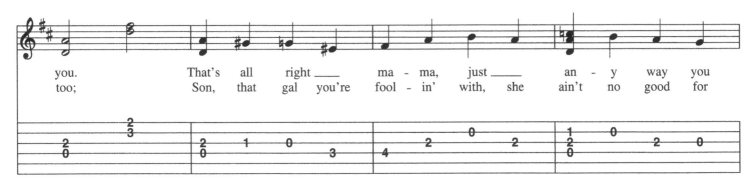

| you. | That's | all | right _____ | ma - ma, | just _____ | an - y | way | you |
| too; | Son, | that | gal you're | fool - in' | with, she | ain't | no good | for |

Chorus

G7

| do. | | | | | | |
| you, but { | That's | all | right, | that's | all | right. _____ |

D

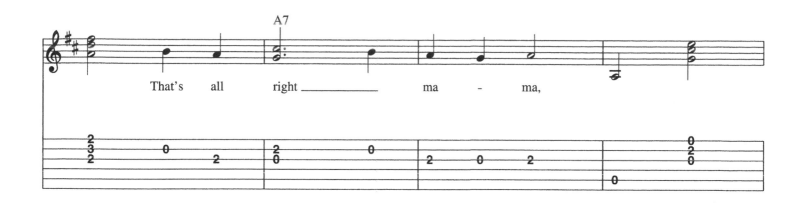

That's all right _____ ma - ma,

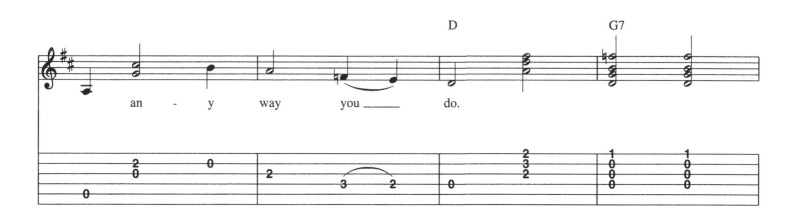

an - y way you ____ do.

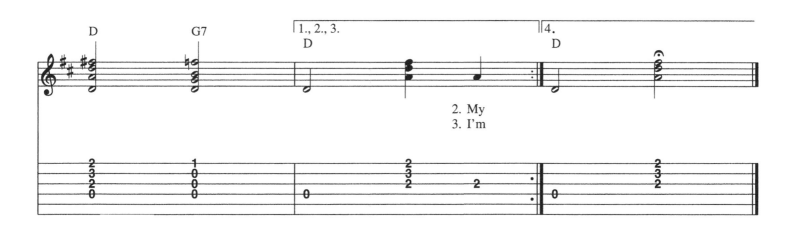

2. My
3. I'm

Additional Lyrics

3. I'm leavin' town now, baby,
   I'm leavin' town for sure.
   Then you won't be bothered with me
   hangin' round your door, but that's all (To Chorus)

4. I oughta mind my papa,
   Guess I'm not too smart.
   If I was I'd let you go
   Before you break my heart, but that's all (To Chorus)

There Goes My Everything

Words and Music by Dallas Frazier

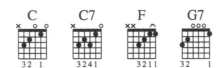

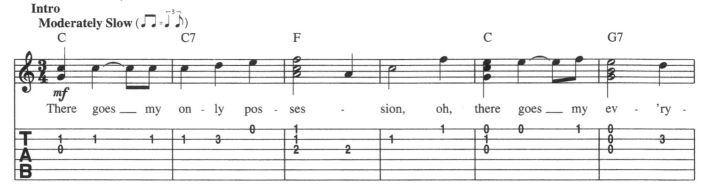

Strum Pattern: 8, 9
Pick Pattern: 7, 8

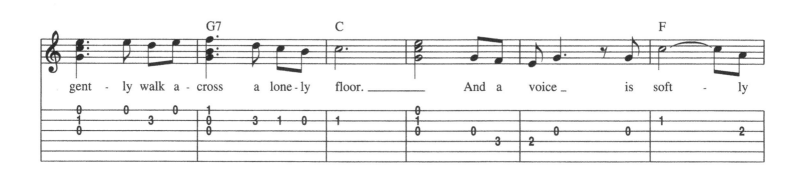

Chorus

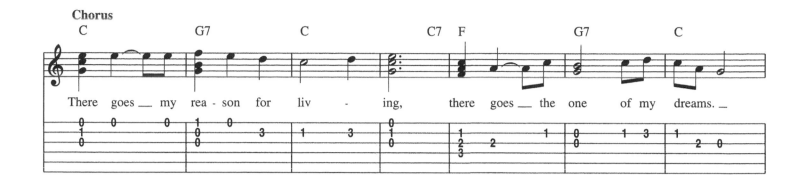

There goes __ my rea-son for liv-__ ing, there goes __ the one of my dreams. __

There goes __ my on-ly pos-ses -__ sion, oh, there goes __ my ev-'ry-

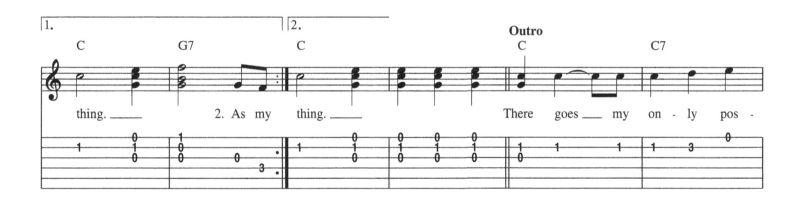

1. thing. _____ 2. As my thing. _____ There goes __ my on-ly pos-

Outro

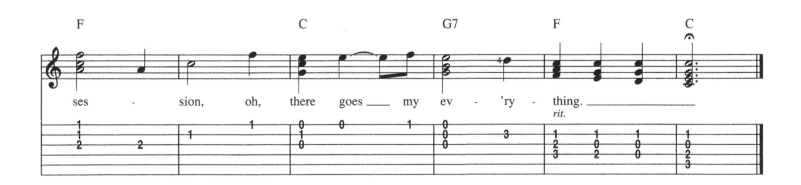

ses -__ sion, oh, there goes __ my ev-'ry-thing. _____
rit.

Additional Lyrics

2. As my mem'ry turns back the pages,
   I can see the happy years we had before.
   Now the love that kept this old heart beating,
   Has been shattered by the closing of the door.

T-R-O-U-B-L-E

Words and Music by Jerry Chesnut

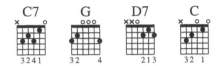

Strum Pattern: 1
Pick Pattern: 2
Verse
Fast Country

1. I play an old pi - an - o from nine till a half past one.

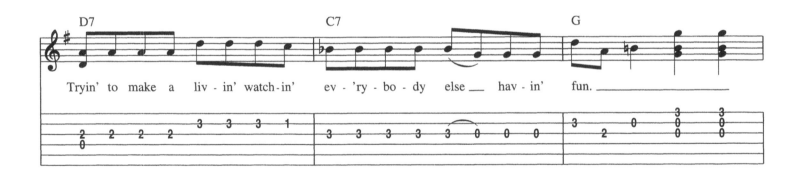

Tryin' to make a liv - in' watch - in' ev - 'ry - bo - dy else ___ hav - in' fun. ___

Well, I don't miss much that ev - er hap - pens on a dance - hall floor. ___

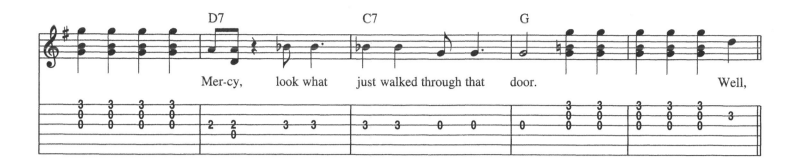

Mer-cy, look what just walked through that door. Well,

Chorus

hel - lo T - R - O - U - B - L - E. ___

What in the world _ you do - in' A - L - O - N - E? Say, hey _

___ good L - dou-ble - O - K - I - N - G, ___

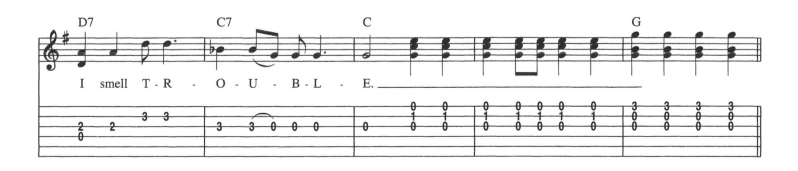

I smell T - R - O - U - B - L - E. ___

Verse

2. I was a lit-tle bit-ty ba-by when my pa-pa hit the skids.
3., 4. *See Additional Lyrics*

Ma-ma had a time tryin' to raise nine kids. Told me not to stare 'cause it was

im-po-lite. And did the best she could to try to raise me right. Hey, but

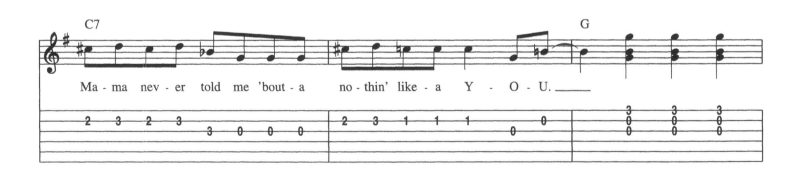

Ma-ma nev-er told me 'bout a no-thin' like a Y - O - U.

Say, your moth-er must a been an-oth-er some-thin' or an-oth-er, too.

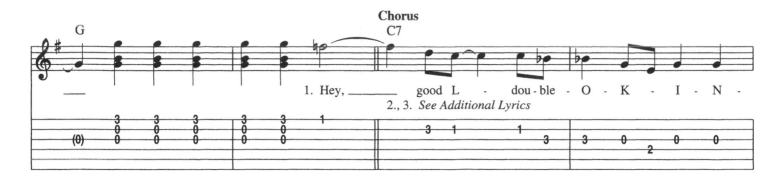

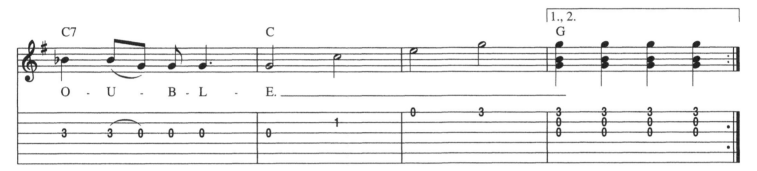

Additional Lyrics

3. Well, you talk about a woman, I've seen a lotta others,
   With too much somethin' and not enough of 'nother.
   They get it all together like a lovin' machine,
   Lookin' like glory and walkin' like a dream.

Chorus 2. Mother Nature's sure been good to Y-O-U.
   Well, your mother musta been another good lookin' mother, too.
   Say, hey! Good L-double-O-K-I-N-G,
   I smell T-R-O-U-B-L-E.

4. Well, you talk about a trouble-makin' hunka pokey bait.
   The men are gonna love, and all the women gonna hate.
   Remindin' them of everything they're never gonna be,
   Maybe the beginnin' of a World War Three.

Chorus 3. 'Cause the world ain't ready for nothin' like a Y-O-U.
   Well, I bet your mother musta been a good lookin' mother, too.
   Say, hey! Good L-double-O-K-I-N-G,
   I smell T-R-O-U-B-L-E.

Wooden Heart

Words and Music by Ben Weisman, Kay Twomey, Fred Wise and Berthold Kaempfert

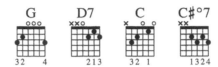

Strum Pattern: 3, 4
Pick Pattern: 3

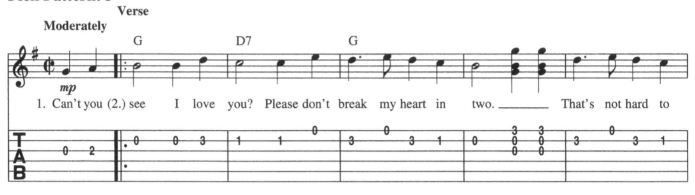

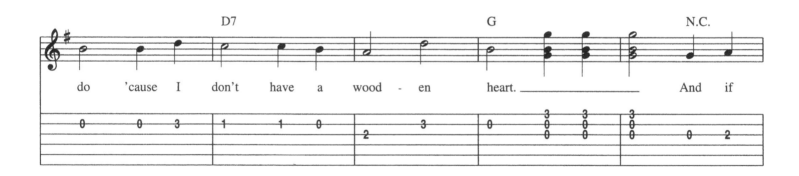

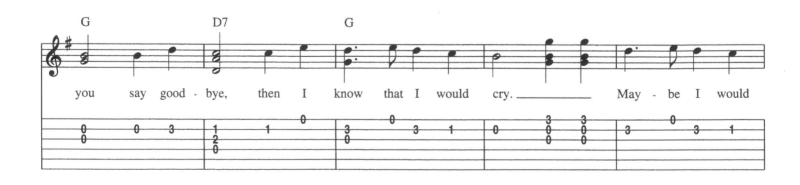

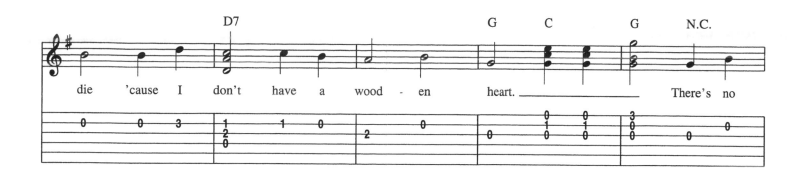

die 'cause I don't have a wood - en heart. _____ There's no

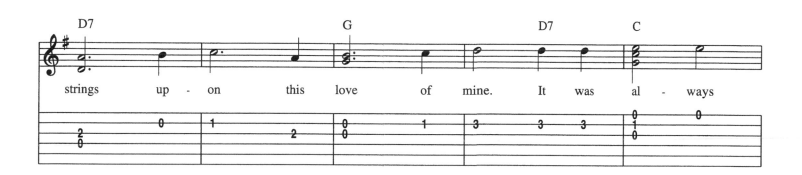

strings up - on this love of mine. It was al - ways

you from the start. _____ Treat me nice, treat me good, treat me

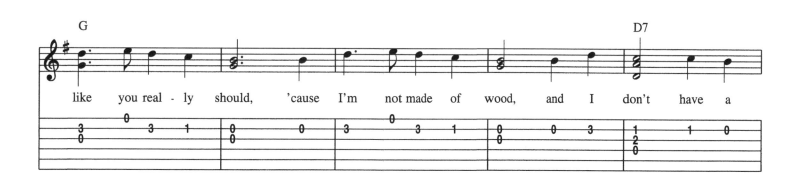

like you real - ly should, 'cause I'm not made of wood, and I don't have a

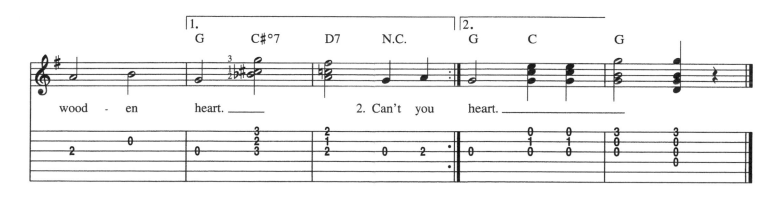

wood - en heart. _____ 2. Can't you heart. _____

EASY GUITAR
WITH NOTES & TAB

This series features simplified arrangements with notes, tab, chord charts, and strum and pick patterns.

MIXED FOLIOS

00702287 Acoustic	$19.99
00702002 Acoustic Rock Hits for Easy Guitar	$15.99
00702166 All-Time Best Guitar Collection	$19.99
00702232 Best Acoustic Songs for Easy Guitar	$16.99
00119835 Best Children's Songs	$16.99
00703055 The Big Book of Nursery Rhymes & Children's Songs	$16.99
00698978 Big Christmas Collection	$19.99
00702394 Bluegrass Songs for Easy Guitar	$15.99
00289632 Bohemian Rhapsody	$19.99
00703387 Celtic Classics	$16.99
00224808 Chart Hits of 2016-2017	$14.99
00267383 Chart Hits of 2017-2018	$14.99
00334293 Chart Hits of 2019-2020	$16.99
00403479 Chart Hits of 2021-2022	$16.99
00702149 Children's Christian Songbook	$9.99
00702028 Christmas Classics	$8.99
00101779 Christmas Guitar	$14.99
00702141 Classic Rock	$8.95
00159642 Classical Melodies	$12.99
00253933 Disney/Pixar's Coco	$16.99
00702203 CMT's 100 Greatest Country Songs	$34.99
00702283 The Contemporary Christian Collection	$16.99

00196954 Contemporary Disney	$19.99
00702239 Country Classics for Easy Guitar	$24.99
00702257 Easy Acoustic Guitar Songs	$17.99
00702041 Favorite Hymns for Easy Guitar	$12.99
00222701 Folk Pop Songs	$17.99
00126894 Frozen	$14.99
00333922 Frozen 2	$14.99
00702286 Glee	$16.99
00702160 The Great American Country Songbook	$19.99
00702148 Great American Gospel for Guitar	$14.99
00702050 Great Classical Themes for Easy Guitar	$9.99
00275088 The Greatest Showman	$17.99
00148030 Halloween Guitar Songs	$14.99
00702273 Irish Songs	$14.99
00192503 Jazz Classics for Easy Guitar	$16.99
00702275 Jazz Favorites for Easy Guitar	$17.99
00702274 Jazz Standards for Easy Guitar	$19.99
00702162 Jumbo Easy Guitar Songbook	$24.99
00232285 La La Land	$16.99
00702258 Legends of Rock	$14.99
00702189 MTV's 100 Greatest Pop Songs	$34.99
00702272 1950s Rock	$16.99
00702271 1960s Rock	$16.99
00702270 1970s Rock	$24.99
00702269 1980s Rock	$16.99

00702268 1990s Rock	$24.99
00369043 Rock Songs for Kids	$14.99
00109725 Once	$14.99
00702187 Selections from O Brother Where Art Thou?	$19.99
00702178 100 Songs for Kids	$16.99
00702515 Pirates of the Caribbean	$17.99
00702125 Praise and Worship for Guitar	$14.99
00287930 Songs from *A Star Is Born, The Greatest Showman, La La Land*, and More Movie Musicals	$16.99
00702285 Southern Rock Hits	$12.99
00156420 Star Wars Music	$16.99
00121535 30 Easy Celtic Guitar Solos	$16.99
00244654 Top Hits of 2017	$14.99
00283786 Top Hits of 2018	$14.99
00302269 Top Hits of 2019	$14.99
00355779 Top Hits of 2020	$14.99
00374083 Top Hits of 2021	$16.99
00702294 Top Worship Hits	$17.99
00702255 VH1's 100 Greatest Hard Rock Songs	$34.99
00702175 VH1's 100 Greatest Songs of Rock and Roll	$34.99
00702253 Wicked	$12.99

ARTIST COLLECTIONS

00702267 AC/DC for Easy Guitar	$16.99
00156221 Adele – 25	$16.99
00396889 Adele – 30	$19.99
00702040 Best of the Allman Brothers	$16.99
00702865 J.S. Bach for Easy Guitar	$15.99
00702169 Best of The Beach Boys	$16.99
00702292 The Beatles — 1	$22.99
00125796 Best of Chuck Berry	$16.99
00702201 The Essential Black Sabbath	$15.99
00702250 blink-182 — Greatest Hits	$17.99
02501615 Zac Brown Band — The Foundation	$17.99
02501621 Zac Brown Band — You Get What You Give	$16.99
00702043 Best of Johnny Cash	$17.99
00702090 Eric Clapton's Best	$16.99
00702086 Eric Clapton — from the Album Unplugged	$17.99
00702202 The Essential Eric Clapton	$17.99
00702053 Best of Patsy Cline	$17.99
00222697 Very Best of Coldplay – 2nd Edition	$17.99
00702229 The Very Best of Creedence Clearwater Revival	$16.99
00702145 Best of Jim Croce	$16.99
00702278 Crosby, Stills & Nash	$12.99
14042809 Bob Dylan	$15.99
00702276 Fleetwood Mac — Easy Guitar Collection	$17.99
00139462 The Very Best of Grateful Dead	$16.99
00702136 Best of Merle Haggard	$16.99
00702227 Jimi Hendrix — Smash Hits	$19.99
00702288 Best of Hillsong United	$12.99
00702236 Best of Antonio Carlos Jobim	$15.99

00702245 Elton John — Greatest Hits 1970–2002	$19.99
00129855 Jack Johnson	$17.99
00702204 Robert Johnson	$16.99
00702234 Selections from Toby Keith — 35 Biggest Hits	$12.95
00702003 Kiss	$16.99
00702216 Lynyrd Skynyrd	$17.99
00702182 The Essential Bob Marley	$16.99
00146081 Maroon 5	$14.99
00121925 Bruno Mars – Unorthodox Jukebox	$12.99
00702248 Paul McCartney — All the Best	$14.99
00125484 The Best of MercyMe	$12.99
00702209 Steve Miller Band — Young Hearts (Greatest Hits)	$12.95
00124167 Jason Mraz	$15.99
00702096 Best of Nirvana	$16.99
00702211 The Offspring — Greatest Hits	$17.99
00138026 One Direction	$17.99
00702030 Best of Roy Orbison	$17.99
00702144 Best of Ozzy Osbourne	$14.99
00702279 Tom Petty	$17.99
00102911 Pink Floyd	$17.99
00702139 Elvis Country Favorites	$19.99
00702293 The Very Best of Prince	$19.99
00699415 Best of Queen for Guitar	$16.99
00109279 Best of R.E.M.	$14.99
00702208 Red Hot Chili Peppers — Greatest Hits	$17.99
00198960 The Rolling Stones	$17.99
00174793 The Very Best of Santana	$16.99
00702196 Best of Bob Seger	$16.99
00146046 Ed Sheeran	$17.99

00702252 Frank Sinatra — Nothing But the Best	$12.99
00702010 Best of Rod Stewart	$17.99
00702049 Best of George Strait	$17.99
00702259 Taylor Swift for Easy Guitar	$15.99
00359800 Taylor Swift – Easy Guitar Anthology	$24.99
00702260 Taylor Swift — Fearless	$14.99
00139727 Taylor Swift — 1989	$19.99
00115960 Taylor Swift — Red	$16.99
00253667 Taylor Swift — Reputation	$17.99
00702290 Taylor Swift — Speak Now	$16.99
00232849 Chris Tomlin Collection – 2nd Edition	$14.99
00702226 Chris Tomlin — See the Morning	$12.95
00148643 Train	$14.99
00702427 U2 — 18 Singles	$19.99
00702108 Best of Stevie Ray Vaughan	$17.99
00279005 The Who	$14.99
00702123 Best of Hank Williams	$15.99
00194548 Best of John Williams	$14.99
00702228 Neil Young — Greatest Hits	$17.99
00119133 Neil Young — Harvest	$14.99

Prices, contents and availability subject to change without notice.

HAL•LEONARD®

Visit Hal Leonard online at **halleonard.com**

0722

306